Mysterious Encounters

The Dover Demon

by Mary Schulte

KIDHAVEN PRESS

A part of Gale, Cengage Learning

GALE
CENGAGE Learning™

Detroit • New York • San Francisco • New Haven, Conn • Waterville, Maine • London

LIBRARY OF CONGRESS CATALOGING-IN-PUBLICATION DATA

Schulte, Mary, 1958-
  The Dover demon / by Mary Schulte.
    p. cm. -- (Mysterious encounters)
  Includes bibliographical references and index.
  ISBN 978-0-7377-4570-2 (hardcover)
  1. Dover demon--Juvenile literature. 2. Cryptozoology--Massachu-
setts--Dover--History--20th century--Juvenile literature. 3. Monsters-
-Massachusetts--Dover--History--20th century--Juvenile literature. 4.
Legends--Massachusetts--Dover--History--20th century--Juvenile literature. 5.
Curiosities and wonders--Massachusetts--Dover--History--20th century--Juvenile lit-
erature. 6. Parapsychology--Massachusetts--Dover--History--20th century--Juvenile
literature. 7. Dover (Mass.)--History--20th century--Juvenile literature. 8. Dover
(Mass.)--Biography--Juvenile literature. I. Title. II. Series.

  QL89.2.D68S38 2010
  001.944--dc22
                                                                2009027450

KidHaven Press
27500 Drake Rd.
Farmington Hills, MI 48331

ISBN-13: 978-0-7377-4570-2
ISBN-10: 0-7377-4570-3

Printed in the United States of America
1 2 3 4 5 6 7 13 12 11 10 09

Printed by Bang Printing, Brainerd, MN, 1ˢᵗ Ptg., 12/2009

Contents

Chapter 1

Who Saw the Dover Demon?

Through the ages, people all over the world have reported seeing strange and unidentifiable creatures. Two of the most famous are Bigfoot, a huge, hairy monster that is said to roam the forests of the Pacific Northwest of the United States, and the Loch Ness Monster, a serpentlike creature some say lives in a lake in Scotland.

Many people believe these sightings are hoaxes, or the result of wild imaginations. The mysterious sightings often cannot be proven true, but no one can prove them untrue either. In 1977 four teenagers in Dover, Massachusetts, saw a creature they could not identify. No one has been able to prove whether the teenagers' eyes just played tricks on

The Loch Ness Monster is another cryptid that, like the Dover Demon, has become a legend through the years.

them in the dark, or if they really had an encounter with a mysterious creature.

One teenager said the creature was shaped like a human baby's body, with long spindly arms and legs. He also described it as having a big, melon-shaped head, about the same size as its crouching body, and glowing orange eyes, but no ears, nose, or mouth.

The second teenager said the creature looked like a monkey, or a small child with an oddly shaped head. He said it walked upright and had glowing orange eyes.

The third teenager said the creature had a big, watermelon-shaped head with glowing green eyes and a tan, hairless body. She saw it crouching be-side the road and guessed it was about the size of a German shepherd. One other teenager saw the creature, but his glance was so brief, he could only say he saw a figure the size of a goat. He could not describe it, and he did not draw a picture of it, as the other three eyewitnesses did. He could only verify that his girlfriend, the third eyewitness, was not making up a story.

Three eyewitnesses, three similar descriptions, three sightings of a mysterious creature that all occurred within 26 hours. What did these teenagers see in Dover, Massachusetts, on April 21 and 22, 1977?

No one else has ever seen this creature that came to be called the "Dover Demon," but it has become a legend along with other unrecognized species, or **cryptids**, such as the Loch Ness Monster, the Abominable Snowman, and Bigfoot.

The First Sighting

Dover, Massachusetts, is a town located about 15 miles (24km) southwest of the state capital of Boston. It has a reputation as the wealthiest town in the state. In 1977 the Dover population was 5,000. The area was fairly rural, with lots of woods and pasture and plenty of space between houses.

At 10:30 P.M. on April 21, 1977, seventeen-year-old Bill Bartlett drove his Volkswagen beetle along Farm Street in Dover. Two friends were with him. Andy Brodie sat in the backseat, and Mike Mazzacca rode in the front passenger seat.

The night was clear and stars blinked in the sky.

Dover, Massachusetts is a fairly rural area, with lots of woods and pasture.

The temperature hovered around 55°F (13°C), enough to cause a shiver, but not really cold.

Off to the left side of the road, Bartlett noticed something creeping on all fours on top of a stone wall. The crouching animal had an egg-shaped head and spindly arms and legs. When his high-beam headlights flashed on it, a hairless creature with orange glowing eyes stared at him, Bartlett reported.

"As I drove by, it turned its head to look at me," Bartlett recalled in an interview. "You get that moment where your eyes meet. I remember that happening. It freaked me out."[1] The encounter scared Bartlett so much that he drove off as fast as he could.

Bartlett's friends were talking to each other and not looking outside. They did not see the creature. After Bartlett drove a safe distance away, he told his friends what he had seen. They convinced him to turn around and go back, so they could see it, too. Brodie and Mazzacca hollered out the window to the creature to show itself. But by then, the mysterious being had vanished.

After he dropped off his friends, Bartlett went home and took out his sketch pad. He then drew a detailed picture of what he saw—a 4-foot-tall (1.2m) creature crouched on a wall. It had a head as

Poltergeists

The Dover Demon sightings were all reported by teenagers. Some people, especially those with a spiritual connection, believe the creature was a poltergeist. A poltergeist is a ghost with a strong aura of spiritual energy that draws it to young people. Poltergeists often move objects, project strange voices, and produce odd electrical effects.

large as its body, orange glowing eyes, and spindly arms and legs.

Bartlett did not remember any other facial features like ears or a nose or a mouth. He said he did not see a tail either. The creature looked naked, with rough skin and "an exaggerated skin color, like Fred Flintstone in the Sunday comics,"[2] Bartlett said at the time.

Later That Night

Around midnight, about an hour and a half after Bartlett's sighting, fifteen-year-old John Baxter, was walking home from visiting his girlfriend. He walked a short way on Millers Hill Road toward Farm Street. He hoped to catch a ride home with someone along the road.

As he walked down the street, he saw a figure coming toward him. He could not see clearly because it was dark, but he thought it might be someone he knew. Baxter called out, but the figure did not answer. Baxter was confused. Why did the figure not respond?

Baxter stopped walking. The figure halted, too. They were about 25 feet (8m) apart, close enough for Baxter to get a better look. He stared at the figure, **mesmerized** by the huge, orange, glowing eyes.

Then the figure dashed down into a gully. Baxter followed it into the woods. The 4-foot-tall (1.2m) creature ran fast for its size. Baxter heard it splash

When John Baxter first saw the Dover Demon he was mesmerized by its huge orange, glowing eyes.

through water, then he saw it hugging a tree on the other side of the stream, about 30 feet away. (Baxter drew the figure in silhouette because it was dark and he could not see details. He described the shape of the creature and the glowing eyes, but did not provide specifics.) At first, he thought that it might be a monkey, but it had no hair.

At that point, Baxter realized he could be in danger. He was alone in the woods, late at night, with a strange creature. Baxter turned around and ran back to the road. Eventually, he caught a ride home.

When Baxter later described what he had seen, it matched the creature that Bartlett saw. The body shape and skinny limbs were the same. The large watermelon-shaped head and orange glowing eyes were described in detail by both teenagers. Bartlett and Baxter denied knowing about each other's meeting with the creature.

The Third Sighting

The next night, around 9:30 P.M., eighteen-year-old William Taintor, was driving with his fifteen-year-old girlfriend, Abby Brabham, near downtown Dover. The temperature was a comfortable 65°F (18°C) under overcast skies.

Suddenly, Brabham saw something crouched on top of a culvert over a stream. The creature had spindly arms and legs and glowing eyes. Brabham's description of the creature matched the previous two eyewitness reports with one major difference—she emphatically described the eyes as green, not orange.

"I know I saw the creature,"[3] she insisted to researchers. Brabham stuck with her claim and said she did not care if people believed her or not.

Taintor had looked over for a

William Taintor and Abby Brabham saw the Dover Demon and described it as a creature about the size of a goat.

International Crypto-zoology Museum

Loren Coleman operates the International Cryptozoology Museum out of his home in Portland, Maine. The most notable artifact is an 8.5-foot-tall (2.5m) stuffed Bigfoot that weighs 500 pounds. Items on display include a small porcelain figurine of the Dover Demon. Coleman also has statues, sculptures, photographs, and figures of other cryptids in the museum.

second and saw something, too, but he could not tell what it was from his brief glimpse. He did confirm Brabham's story that they saw something unrecognizable, a creature about the size of a goat. According to one report, Taintor said he had heard about the mysterious creature from his friend Bill Bartlett earlier that day, but he had not told his girlfriend about it before she saw the creature herself.

Word Gets Out

At first the eyewitnesses did not tell anyone their stories except family and close friends, but word spread fairly quickly through the small town that

News of the creature sightings spread rapidly and soon the town of Dover was filled with radio and television media.

the three teenagers had seen something strange. About a week after the reported sightings, cryptid hunter Loren Coleman, who lived near Dover, stopped in at the Dover Country Store. The cashier mentioned the mysterious creature and said she would get him a copy of Bartlett's drawing.

Coleman was instantly intrigued with the creature he named "Dover Demon." The name was a bit sensational, because there was nothing demonic about the skittish creature. In fact, many people did not believe there had been any sightings at all.

No visible proof of the creature existed. There were no photos, no tracks, and no recorded sounds. The reports by the three eyewitnesses were the only records of its appearance. Coleman took a copy of Bartlett's drawing to the Dover police station in case other witnesses appeared. Several days later, Coleman and the eyewitnesses were interviewed by the *Real Paper* in Cambridge, Massachusetts.

It did not take long for word to get out to radio and television stations about the mysterious creature sightings. Newspapers around the United States, including the Boston *Herald* and the *Boston Globe*, published the news.

Eager to follow up on the incredible story, the media rushed to Dover. Camera crews, reporters, and photographers descended on the Dover area in search of the mysterious being.

Paranormal investigators also swarmed the sites looking for clues. But everyone searched in vain. The mysterious creature had disappeared.

Chapter 2

The Investigation

Cryptid hunter Loren Coleman and three other local men who were recognized **ufologists**, or people who study **UFOs** (unidentified flying objects), worked together to investigate the sightings. They all lived in towns close to Dover and were familiar with the area.

Coleman was a consulting editor of the International Fortean Society and an honorary member of the Society for the Investigation of the Unexplained. Joining him were Joseph Nyman, a member of the Mutual UFO Network and the Aerial Phenomena Research Organization; Ed Fogg of the New England UFO Study Group; and Walter Webb, who was then assistant director of the

Many UFO research groups were interested in the creature sighting, knowing that people would associate the creature with UFOs.

Hayden Planetarium at Boston's Museum of Science. Webb called the sightings, "One of the most baffling creature episodes ever reported."[4]

Even though the creature was not reported to be an alien, no one knew for sure what it was and the researchers were interested in the unexplained **phenomenon**.

Twenty years later Coleman would write the book, *Mysterious America: The Ultimate Guide to the Nation's Weirdest Wonders, Strangest Spots and Creepiest Creatures*. In it he discusses the Dover Demon. Coleman has been contacted by people around the world who want to learn about the mysterious Dover Demon.

Finding the Facts

The investigators went beyond simply questioning the eyewitnesses. They also talked with the parents, teachers, and friends of the teenagers and with local officials. The adults agreed that the young people were honest and trustworthy. The researchers were especially impressed with Bill Bartlett and Abby Brabham. Their sincerity was convincing, and many people, including their parents, supported their trustworthiness. Carl Sheridan, the Dover police chief at the time of the sightings, said, "It was real. Those boys really did see something out there."[5]

Coleman also was convinced that the teenagers had seen something. He believed that the teens were not close friends and that they knew nothing of the other sightings until later. The sight-

Investigators interviewed parents, teachers, and friends to learn if the kids who saw the creature could be trusted.

ings happened during spring vacation, so the teenagers did not have a chance to see each other and compare stories at school.

The investigators carefully documented where the three sightings occurred. They photographed and measured the area that included all three locations, a space of about 2 miles (3.2km). One common factor was that all of the sightings were close to water.

A Thorough Investigation

After gathering information and completing their interviews, the investigators met to review their findings. They determined that Bill Bartlett came within 20 feet (6m) of the creature, and his sighting lasted no more than six seconds. At the time, his car was traveling approximately 40 to 45 miles per hour (64 to 72 km/h). At first glance, Bartlett thought the creature was a cat or a dog. As he stared into the creature's large, glowing eyes, he realized he did not know what it was. "I must confess—at seeing it, I panicked, screamed, and sped off down the road,"[6] Bartlett said.

The fear in Bartlett's voice made his friends believe he had seen something. Although Brodie and Mazzacca persuaded him to go back, they saw no sign of the strange little figure.

Even so, Bartlett provided the best description and a detailed drawing of the creature. His sketch has become the most widely used drawing of the Dover Demon. The drawing has appeared in newspapers and books. It shows the creature on all fours, struggling to climb over a pile of rocks. Its long fingers and toes clutch the rocks, almost molded to the shape of the stones.

The investigators also determined that John Baxter had his bizarre encounter about two hours after Bartlett's. Baxter first noticed the creature about 100 feet (30m) away, according to measurements by the investigators. When Baxter and the creature were about 25 feet (7.6m) apart, they both stopped. The tiny figure then dashed into the woods and Baxter followed. In the drawing he made, Baxter shows the creature standing upright next to a tree. Its long fingers grip the trunk for support. Its strange, long toes are curled around the rocks. Baxter's drawing is quite similar to Bartlett's. Although Baxter was not an artist like Bartlett, he

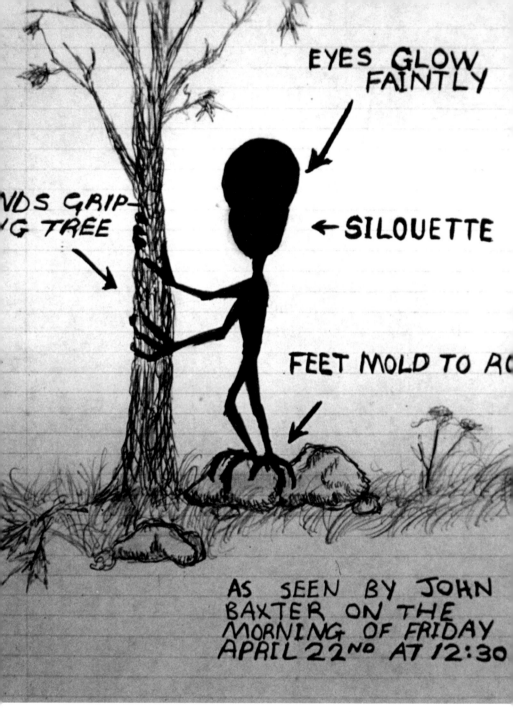

EYES GLOW
FAINTLY

NDS GRIP-
G TREE

← SILOUETTE

FEET MOLD TO RO

AS SEEN BY JOHN
BAXTER ON THE
MORNING OF FRIDAY
APRIL 22ND AT 12:30

The drawing John Baxter made after seeing the Dover Demon. It shows the creature with long, spindly arms standing next to a tree.

did spend more time looking at the creature. Like Bartlett, Baxter made his drawing immediately after seeing the creature, while its image was fresh in his mind.

Brabham and Taintor were possibly within 8 feet (2.4m) of the creature, according to the investigators' measurements. Although Brabham thought she looked at the creature for more than half a minute, the investigators determined it was more like five seconds. Taintor's view of the creature was even shorter. He could not provide much description, other than to say it was about the size of a goat hunched over in the road.

Conflicting Stories

There is some confusion about when each eyewitness learned about the other sightings. According to a report by investigator Nyman, during an interview on May 21, 1977, Taintor said he and Baxter learned about Bartlett's sighting on Friday, April 22. The boys were talking when Bartlett asked if they had heard about what he saw. Baxter chimed in to say he also had seen something the night before. When they compared stories, they realized they were talking about what appeared to be the same creature.

Later that same night, Taintor and Brabham saw the creature. Taintor said he had not told his girlfriend about the sightings by the other two boys.

According to investigator Webb's report, when

Baxter was interviewed by investigators on May 21, he said he learned about Bartlett's sighting and his drawing about five days after the sightings. Baxter was showing his classmates his drawing, when someone commented that it looked just like the creature Bartlett drew.

On another occasion Bartlett said he could not remember for sure when he first saw Baxter's drawing. It might have been that Friday, April 22, or perhaps not until they saw each other at a party Saturday night. Investigator Coleman stated that he believes the eyewitnesses did not learn of the other sightings until the next week at school. The three different claims for when the boys learned about the sightings and their changing stories led some people to doubt their stories.

Another unanswered question is: How well did the eyewitnesses know each other? Nyman's report says that Bartlett and Baxter knew of each other because they were students at the same school, but that was all. Bartlett and Taintor were good friends, however. Their friendship made some people question the believability of their reported sightings.

Was It a Hoax?

Some Dover residents thought the teenagers were making up the stories. Others thought maybe someone else played a practical joke on the teens for fun. But the police chief disagreed. He said, "That thing has haunted me for 29 years. I knew

Unlike a chupacabra, shown here, which has been spotted many places in the world, the Dover Demon is unique and not connected to other paranormal creatures.

the kids involved. They were good kids . . . pretty reliable kids."[7]

Bartlett's friends who were in the car with him said their friend was terrified of what he had seen. The young man's parents agreed. His father told investigators that his son was extremely upset when he came home. The parents also said their son was not the kind of kid who made up stories or played pranks. After Bartlett told his father what he had seen, the teen immediately went in his room to draw a picture of the creature.

Baxter was less convincing. He was a science-fiction buff, who wrote his own fantasy stories. Although his parents believed he saw "something," his father was concerned that his son's interest in science fiction could have influenced his sighting.

In his report investigator Webb wrote, "The Dover Demon is a disturbing, bizarre affair. There are many frustrating, troublesome aspects about it. But despite the doubts and questions this episode raises, I believe a hoax is unlikely."[8]

Coleman says the Dover Demon has stayed in people's minds because it is unique. No one else has reported seeing such a creature anywhere else in the world. Although some people try to draw comparisons, "the Dover Demon does not resemble a chupacabra or an alien like the Roswell aliens or the bat-eared goblins of Hopkinsville, Kentucky," says Coleman. "It's extremely unique. It has no real connections to any other inexplicable phenomena."[9]

Other Explanations

Many people have tried to explain what the teenagers may have seen. Some say it could have been an undiscovered natural species or a **mutation** or a **hybrid**. Others suggest that the eyewitnesses saw a monkey, a goat, a foal, or a fox.

At the time, one of the most popular theories was that it was a newborn foal. That would explain the spindly legs and perhaps the color. But inves-

Chupacabras

Chupacabras are legendary blood-sucking cryptids. Its name comes from the Spanish words *chupar* (to suck) and *cabra* (goat), so its literal name is "goat sucker." First sighted in Puerto Rico, chupacabras have also been spotted in Mexico and the United States. They are about the size of a small bear, with a row of spines from the neck to the tail.

tigators did not find any animal tracks or animal remains in the area. No one reported a missing newborn foal either. And, Baxter's description of the creature standing upright would make a four-legged animal unlikely.

Bartlett does not know what the creature was, but he is positive about what it was not. "It wasn't a fox or some other animal,"[10] he declared. He grew up in Dover, and he was familiar with the local animals.

Could it have been a creature from another world? The alien-like appearance and late-night sightings of the mysterious creature that was never seen again make the suggestion of an **extraterrestrial** almost believable.

Chapter 3

Mysterious New England

New England has a history of mystery. Many of the towns in New England are very old. They date back to Colonial times. Stories of ghosts, haunted houses, sea monsters, witches, and strange phenomena make Massachusetts a treasure trove of fantastical tales. In her book, *Haunted Massachusetts: Ghosts and Strange Phenomena of the Bay State,* author Cheri Revai calls the state, "The most spirit-laden region in the entire country."[11] The Dover Demon is one of the state's most famous **enigmas**.

Farm Street

Bill Bartlett first spotted the Dover Demon as

he drove along Farm Street. Long ago, the street was an Indian trail. It is the second-oldest road in Dover, but the first one that was named. In 1680 resident John Battle nailed a board to a tree and painted "Farm Street" on it.

According to cryptid hunter Loren Coleman, the Farm Street area has a tradition of unexplained activity that dates to the 1700s. He says, "It's almost as if there are certain areas that 'collect' sightings, almost in a magnetic way."[12]

"In the same area you had three major legends going on,"[13] he says, listing a sighting of the devil on horseback, reports of buried treasure, and the Dover Demon.

The 1914 book, *Dover Farms*, written by Frank Smith, notes a local farmer's mysterious sighting

Bridgewater Triangle

The Bridgewater Triangle is a 200-square-mile (518sq. km) patch of swamp and towns in southeast Massachusetts. Students of the paranormal consider the area a top spot for mysterious creature sightings. Within the borders of the triangle, people have reported seeing UFOs, Bigfoot-type creatures, and the ghosts of crazed truck drivers.

on Farm Street centuries ago. Smith writes, "Amid the superstitions of the age he thought he saw his Satanic Majesty [the devil] as he was riding on horseback by this secluded spot."[14]

The sightings and spirited references to the Farm Street area give it a mysterious reputation. Coleman compares the strange occurrences in the Dover area with the Bridgewater Triangle in southeast Massachusetts, a top spot for mysterious creature sightings. He says the triangle is where "you find a concentration of weirdness."[15]

New England's Other Famous Cryptids

The Dover Demon is not the only famous cryptid in New England. Bigfoot has been reported in New York and large, black pantherlike creatures supposedly roam New Hampshire. Perhaps the most popular cryptid in the New England area is Champ, a 20-foot (6m), serpentlike monster that reportedly lives at the bottom of Lake Champlain in Vermont.

Lake Champlain is one of the largest bodies of water in the United States, after the Great Lakes. It is almost 110 miles (161km) long and 13 miles (21km) wide. In places, it is 400 feet (122m) deep. Glaciers long ago dug out the lake, where the frigid water seems to be a perfect habitat for a monster hideaway.

Champ is said to resemble a plesiosaur, an ex-

The most popular cyptid that lives in New England is Champ, a serpentlike creature that reportedly lives in Lake Champlain.

tinct water reptile with flippers. The first sighting was more than 300 years ago, and there have been more than 300 sightings since then. Although Champ has not been officially **verified**, the creature is protected by state law. Legislation passed in the 1980s makes it illegal to harm Champ.

Sandra Mansi snapped a photograph that supposedly shows Champ in the lake in 1977. Mansi and her family were picnicking at the lake. The fuzzy, instamatic photo shows the creature's head and long, snakelike neck. Like Bill Bartlett and his sighting of the Dover Demon, Mansi did not seek publicity for her sighting and photo. It was three years before she told anyone about them. The photo was examined by experts, such as George Zug of the Smithsonian National Institute of Natural History, and declared to be unaltered. It supported the existence of something in the lake, but no one knows exactly what. Champ still remains an **elusive** mystery.

The Mannegishi

New England has a water spirit that has been compared with the Dover Demon in appearance. The Cree Indians of Canada talk about a race of little creatures called mannegishi, or maymaygwashi. The mannegishi are mythical beings that live in water or near it. They like to play tricks on travelers. They even go so far as to tip over canoes and small boats to drown people.

The Cree legends say the mannegishi are humanlike, with very thin and spindly arms and legs.

Both the Dover Demon and the Mannegishi have thin spindly arms and legs and oversized heads like this creature.

They have oversize heads with immense eyes, but no nose or mouth. They are similar to Bill Bartlett's description of the Dover Demon. The main difference is that the mannegishi have six fingers on each hand.

Another characteristic of the mannegishi is that they do not have gills or lungs. They get oxygen directly from the air or water around them through their skin. Some people believe the mannegishi communicate by **telepathy**.

Was It an Alien?

Although the physical description of the Dover Demon often draws comparison to the mannegishi, other people suggest that the creature was an alien from a UFO. The figure-eight shape of the Dover Demon's oversize head, slender body, and glow-

Some people suggest that the Dover Demon, with its slender body and large head, is actually an alien from a UFO.

ing eyes resemble what most humans think aliens look like. However, there were no reports of UFO activity anywhere in the area on those two nights in 1977. None of the eyewitnesses reported seeing a UFO.

Coleman says that the year 1977 had an unusually high number of strange events. UFOs and mysterious creatures were frequently sighted, and they appeared to be related. The monsters that were reported often resembled humans. People questioned if the mysterious beings could be visitors from other worlds.

As for the Dover Demon, whatever it was, it was never seen again.

Chapter 4

The Dover Demon Legacy

More than 30 years have passed since the Dover Demon appeared to four teenagers in the small Massachusetts town of Dover. On Halloween Bill Bartlett, who first saw the Dover Demon, often gets phone calls from people who remember his story about the mysterious creature.

In a 2006 interview, Bartlett said he sometimes wishes he had never mentioned that he saw the creature. He does not want to be remembered for his late-night encounter.

"In a lot of ways it's kind of embarrassing to me," he said. "I definitely saw something. It was definitely weird. I didn't make it up. Sometimes I wish I had."[16]

Bartlett knew at the time that it was a story people would have trouble believing. On the detailed sketch he drew that night in 1977, he wrote, "I, Bill Bartlett, swear on a stack of Bibles that I saw this creature."[17]

Anniversary Events

Thirty years to the day after the first Dover Demon sighting, *Spooky Southwest*, a radio program about the paranormal, broadcast a show about the

The Dover Historical Society made Dover Demon T-shirts with this famous sketch made by Bill Bartlett after he saw the creature.

Mothman

A cryptid first spotted in West Virginia in 1966, Mothman was reported as a 7-foot-tall (2.1m), humanlike figure with glowing red eyes and wings folded against its back. Mothman could fly at high speeds, supposedly speeding alongside cars. A 2002 movie, *The Mothman Prophecies* starring Richard Gere and Laura Linney, is based on the creature, which has been reported in many locations around the world. Some people believe Mothman appears shortly before disaster strikes.

creature on the night of April 21, 2007. Host Tim Weisberg interviewed Loren Coleman and other paranormal researchers. The show also featured correspondents at the locations in Dover where the creature was seen. Despite their attention, the Dover Demon did not show up to be interviewed.

To commemorate the 30-year anniversary of the sightings, the Dover Historical Society had T-shirts made. The shirts were printed with Bartlett's famous sketch and the words "Do you believe?" They were sold during the Dover Days Fair in May 2007 as a fund-raiser for the historical society. The

100 adult-size shirts sold-out within 25 minutes and 200 children's shirts sold-out shortly after that. The Dover Demon is a popular icon in its hometown.

A Popular Creature

Although the Dover Demon was seen just briefly by only four people over 30 years ago, it remains a popular creature. The Web site About.com has the Dover Demon on their "Top 10 Most Mysterious Creatures of Modern Times" list.

In a poll of the "Top Ten Supernatural Monsters of All Time," compiled by Brad Steiger in 2006 for *Fate Magazine*, the Dover Demon ranked number ten, even though many of the other creatures on the list have reportedly been seen more than once.

The Dover Demon shows up in other places, too. Japanese toy makers created a

The comic *Proof* follows a Sasquatch, like this one, and his partner as they investigate cryptids, including the chupacabra and the Dover Demon.

Close Encounters of the Third Kind

In 1977, the same year as the Dover Demon sightings, the science-fiction movie *Close Encounters of the Third Kind* was released. Written and directed by Steven Spielberg, it is one of the most popular movies about UFOs ever made. The aliens in the movie share some characteristics with the Dover Demon, such as their childlike bodies, oversize heads, and huge eyes.

plastic figurine of the creature. The Dover Demon is a character in the video game *Hikyou Tanken-tai: Choutoko Special.* Players take control of three **cryptozoologists**, who hunt all sorts of strange creatures, including Bigfoot, Mothman, the Dover Demon, Owlman, the Jersey Devil, and the Loch Ness Monster.

Created by Image Comics in October 2007, the comic book, *Proof* follows the adventures of Special Agents John "Proof" Prufrock (a **Sasquatch**) and his partner Ginger Brown. They work for a secret government organization where their job is to track and investigate strange cryptids. The story lines include encounters with chupacabras, the Dover Demon, and fairies.

Television programs that have featured the Dover Demon include *The X-Files* and *Unsolved Mysteries.*

Newest Theories

A new investigation into the Dover Demon sightings occurred in the 1990s. Martin S. Kottmeyer, a farmer and ufologist from Illinois, suggests that the creature was a young moose. Kottmeyer says that the sightings happened at night in the dark, so

An investigation into the Dover Demon by Martin Kottmeyer theorized that the creature's head shape implies that it was a moose not a cryptid.

the eyewitnesses could not see well. The creature's head shape and lack of facial features could have been the shape of a moose head because a moose's nose and mouth are far down on its muzzle.

Coleman disputes Kottmeyer's theory. He says a moose at that time of year would have been huge, not a small, spindly legged creature. He also argues that moose are **diurnal** animals. They are active at dawn, dusk, and sometimes during the middle of the day, but not at night.

Coleman checked with a wildlife agency to ask about moose sightings in the Dover area. He was told that only two moose had been spotted in Massachusetts during the year of the Dover Demon sighting. The cases were recorded in western and central Massachusetts in the month of September, far away from the Dover Demon in time and location.

Other people have linked the sightings to ghost stories or fairy tales. Cryptozoologist Mark Hall suggests that the Dover Demon is a pygmy mer-being, a member of the mermaid family.

In the end, the theories are just guesses because no one knows for sure. The Dover Demon remains a mystery. Coleman concludes, "The Dover Demon is a true enigma, an animate anomaly [something unusual] that intersected the lives of four credible young people that lonely week in April, 1977."[18]

Notes

Chapter 1: Who Saw the Dover Demon?

1. Quoted in Kyle Alspach, "'Demon' Bewitches Still, 30 Years Later," *Boston.com*, April 22, 2007, www.boston.com/news/local/articles/2007/04/22/demon_bewitches_still_30_years_later.
2. Quoted in Loren Coleman, *Mysterious America: The Ultimate Guide to the Nation's Weirdest Wonders, Strangest Spots and Creepiest Creatures*. New York: Paraview Pocket Books, 2007, p. 46.
3. Coleman, *Mysterious America*, p. 52.

Chapter 2: The Investigation

4. Quoted in Joseph Citro, *Passing Strange: True Tales of New England Hauntings and Horrors*. Boston, MA: Houghton Mifflin, 1996, p. 136.
5. Quoted in Citro, *Passing Strange*, p. 143.
6. Quoted in Joseph A. Citro and Mark Sceurman, *Weird New England*. New York: Sterling, 2005, p. 107.
7. Quoted in Mark Sullivan, "Decades Later, the Dover Demon Still Haunts," *Boston.com*, October 29, 2006, www.boston.com/news/local/articles/2006/10/29/decades_later_the_dover_demon_still_haunts.
8. Quoted in Coleman, *Mysterious America*, p. 56.
9. Quoted in Sullivan, "Decades Later, the Dover Demon Still Haunts."
10. Quoted in Alspach, "'Demon' Bewitches Still, 30 Years Later."

Chapter 3: Mysterious New England

11. Cheri Revai, *Haunted Massachusetts: Ghosts and Strange Phenomena of the Bay State.* Mechanicsburg, PA: Stackpole, 2005, p. 2.

12. Quoted in Sullivan, "Decades Later, the Dover Demon Still Haunts."

13. Quoted in Sullivan, "Decades Later, the Dover Demon Still Haunts."

14. Frank Smith, *Dover Farms.* Dover, Massachusetts: The Historical and Natural History Society, 1914, p. 8.

15. Quoted in Tim Weisberg, *Spooky Southcoast*, Radio program from April 21, 2007, radio 1480 New Bedford, Mass.

Chapter 4: The Dover Demon Legacy

16. Quoted in Sullivan, "Decades Later, the Dover Demon Still Haunts."

17. Quoted in Sullivan, "Decades Later, the Dover Demon Still Haunts."

18. Coleman, *Mysterious America*, p. 61.

Glossary

cryptids: Unidentified, mysterious animals.

cryptozoologists: Researchers of hidden, unknown, or unverified species or animals.

diurnal: Active during the daytime rather than at night.

elusive: Difficult to find or catch.

enigmas: Things that are puzzling or unable to be explained.

extraterrestrial: A life form that exists outside of Earth or its atmosphere.

hybrid: Something produced from a mixture of two unrelated things.

mesmerized: Fixed attention, as if under a spell.

mutation: A change or alteration of form.

paranormal: Beyond normal scientific explanation.

phenomenon: An unusual or significant happening.

Sasquatch: Another name for Bigfoot, also known as Yeti.

telepathy: Communicating from one mind to another without speaking.

UFOs: Unidentified flying objects.

ufologists: People who study UFOs.

verified: Proved to be true.

For Further Exploration

Books

Loren Coleman, *Mysterious America: The Ultimate Guide to the Nation's Weirdest Wonders, Strangest Spots and Creepiest Creatures*. New York: Paraview Pocket Books, 2007. Written by one of the original investigators of the Dover Demon sightings, this guidebook tells about creatures and phantoms and the stories of those who saw them.

Scott Francis, *Monster Spotter's Guide to North America*. Cincinnati, OH: How Books, 2007. This is a tongue-in-cheek guide to finding monsters that includes suggestions for a "monster spotters tool kit."

Kelly Milner Halls, Rick Spears, and Roxyanne Young. *Tales of the Cryptids: Mysterious Creatures that May or May Not Exist*. Darby Creek Publishing, 2006. Drawings, maps, and photographs illustrate this book of fascinating creatures from modern times back to prehistoric times with an alphabetical "criptidictionary" to keep them in order.

Cheri Revai, *Haunted Massachusetts: Ghosts and Strange Phenomena of the Bay State*. Mechanicsburg, PA: Stackpole, 2005. This book offers dozens of stories about the ghosts and haunted areas of Massachusetts, grouped by location.

Rory Storm, *Monster Hunt: The Guide to Cryptozoology*. New York: Sterling, 2008. A good beginner's guide to monsters and unknown creatures that lists the monsters by geographic location.

Shannon R. Turlington, Cheryl Kimball, and Christel A. Shea, *The Everything Kids' Monsters Book*. Avon, MA: Adams Media Corporation, 2002. Beginner's guide to monsters and ancient creatures that also includes puzzles and games.

Internet Source

Mark Sullivan, "Decades Later, the Dover Demon Still Haunts," *Boston.com*, October 29, 2006, www.boston.com/news/local/articles/2006/10/29/decades_later_the_dover_demon_still_haunts.

Web Sites

Cryptomundo (www.cryptomundo.com). This Web site is devoted to news and discussions about cryptids.

Strange New England (http://strangene.com/monsters/dover.htm). This ezine explores the mysterious creatures and strange legends of the New England area.

Index

Picture Credits

About the Author

Mary Schulte is the author of many stories and articles that have been published in magazines, such as *Highlights, Highlights High Five, Ladybug,* and *My Friend.* She has written one fiction book and twelve nonfiction books, including *Minotaur* and *Sirens* for KidHaven Press's Monsters series. Schulte lives in Kansas City, Missouri, where she works as a photo editor and children's book reviewer at the *Kansas City Star* when she is not chasing after her household demons—three children, three dogs, two cats, and a bird.